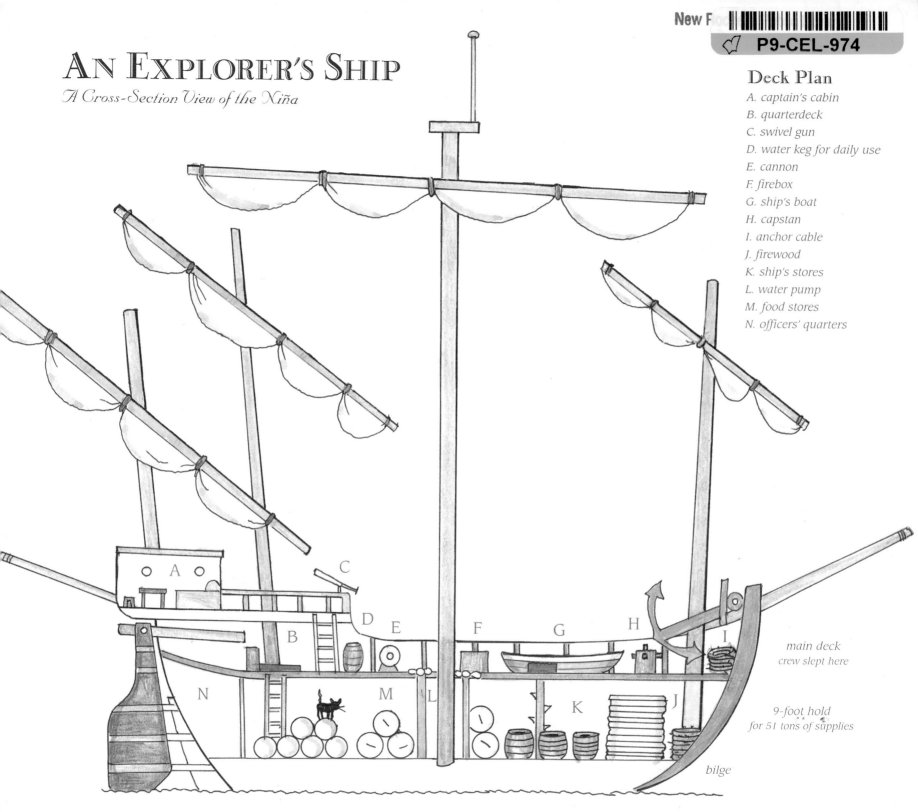

AN EXPLORER'S SHIP
A Cross-Section View of the Niña

Deck Plan
A. captain's cabin
B. quarterdeck
C. swivel gun
D. water keg for daily use
E. cannon
F. firebox
G. ship's boat
H. capstan
I. anchor cable
J. firewood
K. ship's stores
L. water pump
M. food stores
N. officers' quarters

main deck
crew slept here

9-foot hold
for 51 tons of supplies

bilge

JAN -- '05

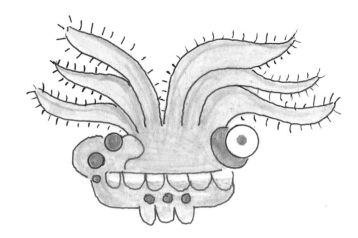

"*Revere and greet your elders; console the poor and the afflicted with good works and words. . . . Do not mock the old, the sick, the maimed, or one who has sinned. . . . Do not set a bad example, or speak indiscreetly, or interrupt the speech of another. If someone does not speak well or coherently, see that you do not do the same; if it is not your business to speak, be silent.*"

—A FATHER'S ADVICE TO HIS
SON, FROM PRE-COLUMBIAN
AZTEC WRITING

"*We suffer from a disease that only gold can cure.*"

—SPANISH EXPLORER AND SOLDIER
HERNÁN CORTÉS, 1485–1547

LAND HO!

*Fifty Glorious Years in the Age of Exploration
with 12 Important Explorers*

written and illustrated by
Nancy Winslow Parker

HarperCollins Publishers

Christopher Columbus's

COAT OF ARMS

Kingdom of Castile

Kingdom of Leon

*islands of the New World
discovered by Columbus*

*anchors represent title of
admiral of the ocean sea*

*Columbus's
personal emblem*

*This book is dedicated to the Most Reverend Desmond Mpilo Tutu,
archbishop emeritus of Cape Town, retired, an "explorer" in the
realms of truth and reconciliation.*

Page 11: inset based on Waldseemüller world map, 1507. Page 17: inset based on sixteenth-century engraving. Page 23: based on a 1795 map of New Britain. Page 27: inset based on a 1598 map. Pages 30–31: based on Battista Agnese map, 1544

Land Ho! Copyright © 2001 by Nancy Winslow Parker Printed in the U.S.A. All rights reserved. www.harperchildrens.com

Library of Congress Cataloging-in-Publication Data   Parker, Nancy Winslow.   Land Ho! Fifty Glorious Years in the Age of Exploration with 12 Important Explorers / written and illustrated by Nancy Winslow Parker.
p.   cm.   Summary: Explains how the voyages of Columbus, Cabot, Ponce De Leon, and other European explorers to the American continents were the result of mistakes, accidents, and misses and discusses the explorers' cruel treatment of native peoples.   ISBN 0-06-027759-9. — ISBN 0-06-027760-2 (lib. bdg.)   1. Explorers—Juvenile literature. [1. Explorers. 2. America—Discovery and exploration.] I. Title.
G175.P3375 2000   99-23006   910'.92'2—dc21   CIP   [B]

Typography by Becky James   1 2 3 4 5 6 7 8 9 10 ❖ First Edition

～ WHERE TO FIND THE EXPLORERS ～

EXPLORER	SAILS UNDER THE FLAG OF	PAGE
Christopher Columbus	Spain	4
John Cabot	England	6
Amerigo Vespucci	Spain/Portugal	8
Vasco Núñez de Balboa	Spain	10
Juan Ponce de León	Spain	12
Ferdinand Magellan	Spain	14
Giovanni da Verrazano	France	16
Alvar Núñez Cabeza de Vaca	Spain	18
Jacques Cartier	France	20
Hernando de Soto	Spain	22
Francisco Vásquez de Coronado	Spain	24
Juan Rodríguez Cabrillo	Spain	26

THE EXPLORERS

Today we know where all the continents are. But this was not always so. For thousands of years North and South America were unknown to Europeans, Asians, or Africans. When the Vikings, led by Leif Eriksson, landed on the shores of North America in the eleventh century, they called their settlement Vineland, because of the grapevines they found growing there. But there were no signs telling them whether they had landed on a continent or just a very big island.

It would be another four hundred years before Europeans landed again in America. This time, ships were faster than they'd ever been, and new navigational instruments helped sailors know where they were on the seas—and how to go back and forth between home and new ports. The explorers wandered up and down the coastlines of North and South America and ventured into their interiors. The extent of their discoveries has led some people to call this period, from 1492 to 1543, the golden age of exploration.

The first two explorers discussed in this book weren't looking for a new continent when they set sail. They were looking for a sea route to the East, to find gold and rare

Leif Eriksson

John Cabot

Giovanni da Verrazano

Jacques Cartier

spices for their kings and queens. But once they realized they had stumbled upon two new continents, they decided to look around some more.

In fifty years, the explorers discovered countless Indian tribes, a new ocean (the Pacific), rivers, plants, animals, and geographical wonders. They altered some cultures and destroyed others. Many explorers died on their voyages; a few lucky ones made it home as rich men.

And they changed the map of the world forever.

Francisco Vásquez
de Coronado

Juan Rodríguez
Cabrillo

Hernando de Soto

Amerigo Vespucci

Alvar Núñez
Cabeza de Vaca

Vasco Núñez
de Balboa

Christopher Columbus

Ferdinand Magellan

Juan Ponce de León

3

CHRISTOPHER COLUMBUS, 1451–1506

Italian Explorer in the Service of Spain

Christoforo Colombo, now known as Christopher Columbus, was sent by King Ferdinand and Queen Ysabella of Spain to find a western route to China (then called Cathay) and the Indies (India, Indochina, and the East Indies). In 1492 Columbus sailed west with the *Niña*, the *Pinta*, and the *Santa Maria* into the sandy islands of the Bahamas. Columbus thought he had found the Indies, and so he called all the natives he saw Indians.

Columbus would make three more voyages and land on many other islands off the coast of North America. He brought back fabulous new fruits and plants, such as corn, tobacco, and potatoes, but it would be about eight more years before Europeans realized that Columbus had stumbled upon a vast new land that would double the size of the known world.

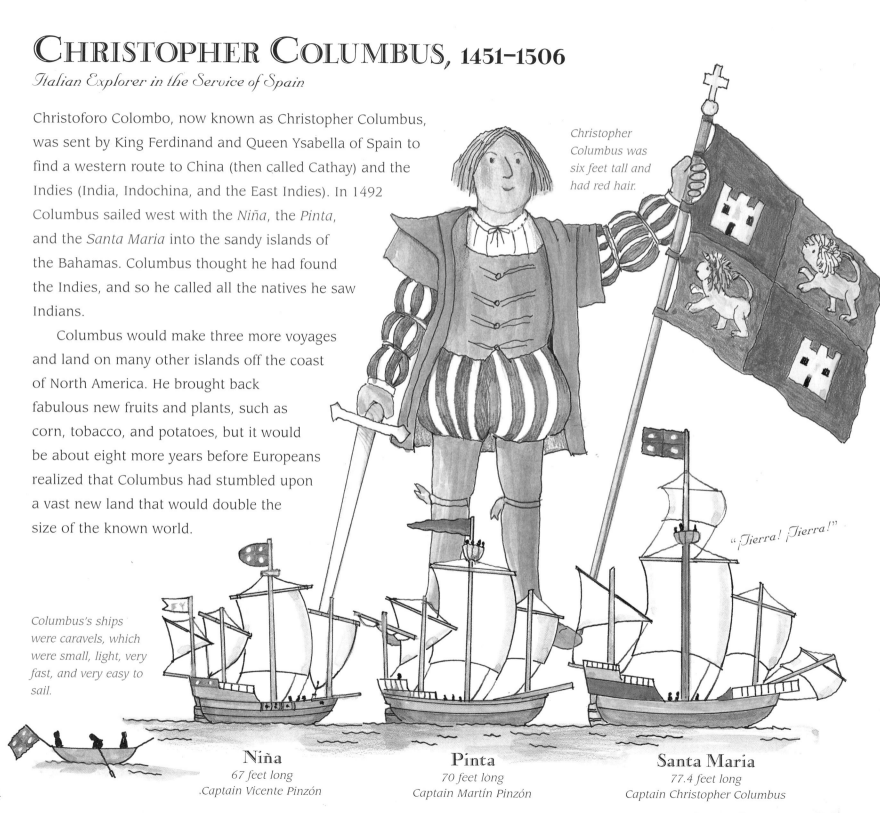

Christopher Columbus was six feet tall and had red hair.

"¡Tierra! ¡Tierra!"

Columbus's ships were caravels, which were small, light, very fast, and very easy to sail.

Niña
67 feet long
Captain Vicente Pinzón

Pinta
70 feet long
Captain Martín Pinzón

Santa Maria
77.4 feet long
Captain Christopher Columbus

THE FOUR VOYAGES OF CHRISTOPHER COLUMBUS

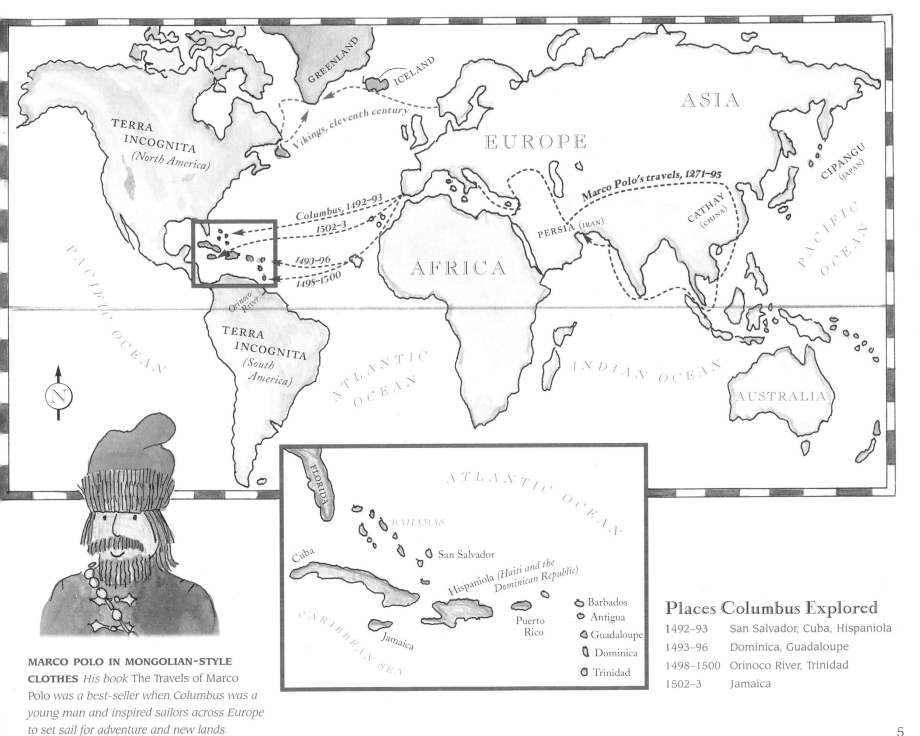

GREENLAND

ICELAND

ASIA

TERRA INCOGNITA
(North America)

EUROPE

Vikings, eleventh century

Marco Polo's travels, 1271–95

CIPANGU
(JAPAN)

Columbus, 1492–93

1502–3

CATHAY
(CHINA)

PERSIA (IRAN)

1493–96

1498–1500

AFRICA

PACIFIC OCEAN

PACIFIC OCEAN

Orinoco River

TERRA INCOGNITA
(South America)

ATLANTIC OCEAN

INDIAN OCEAN

AUSTRALIA

N

ATLANTIC OCEAN

FLORIDA

BAHAMAS

San Salvador

Cuba

Hispaniola (Haiti and the Dominican Republic)

Barbados

Antigua

Guadaloupe

Puerto Rico

Dominica

Jamaica

Trinidad

CARIBBEAN SEA

**MARCO POLO IN MONGOLIAN-STYLE
CLOTHES** *His book* The Travels of Marco
Polo *was a best-seller when Columbus was a
young man and inspired sailors across Europe
to set sail for adventure and new lands.*

Places Columbus Explored

1492–93	San Salvador, Cuba, Hispaniola
1493–96	Dominica, Guadaloupe
1498–1500	Orinoco River, Trinidad
1502–3	Jamaica

JOHN CABOT, 1450?–1499?
Italian Explorer in the Service of England

While the Spanish and Portuguese monarchies were sending their explorers west to find trade routes to the East, England's King Henry VII sent Giovanni Caboto, better known as John Cabot, north instead.

Like Columbus, Cabot never discovered what he was looking for. Instead, he ended up on the shores of the continent the Vikings had found. From there he followed the coastline south and claimed land for England from Nova Scotia all the way to New Jersey. He found no silks, no spices, no gold . . . but he did find lots of fish, especially the plentiful Iceland cod. He also discovered the Grand Banks, which are still considered among the greatest fishing grounds in the world.

Cabot's explorations on behalf of King Henry VII opened up the way for England's colonization of North America. Soon colonies would be established along the entire eastern coastline on behalf of the English monarch.

John Cabot's son, Sebastian, accompanied Cabot on his first voyage.

John Cabot was born in Italy. His favorite books were The Travels of Marco Polo *and the journals of Christopher Columbus.*

The Iceland Cod
2' to 4' long; weighs up to 100 pounds

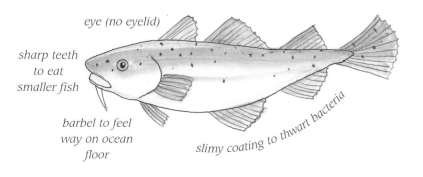

eye (no eyelid)

sharp teeth to eat smaller fish

barbel to feel way on ocean floor

slimy coating to thwart bacteria

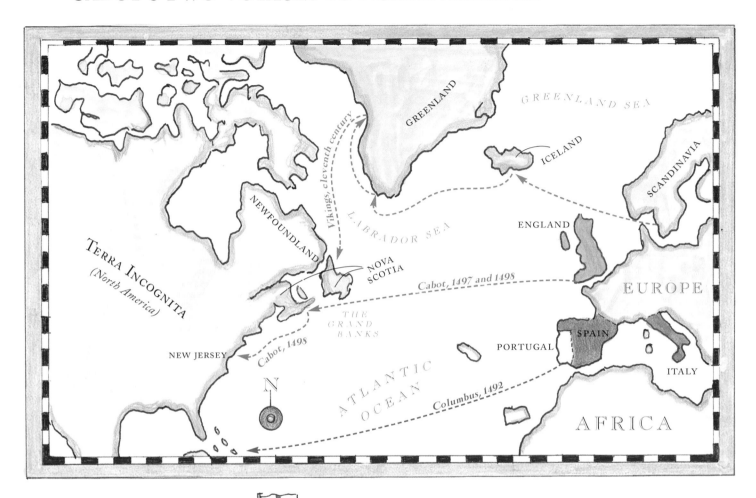

TERRA INCOGNITA
(North America)

GREENLAND

GREENLAND SEA

ICELAND

SCANDINAVIA

Vikings, eleventh century

NEWFOUNDLAND

LABRADOR SEA

NOVA SCOTIA

ENGLAND

EUROPE

Cabot, 1497 and 1498

THE GRAND BANKS

SPAIN

PORTUGAL

ITALY

NEW JERSEY

Cabot, 1498

N

ATLANTIC OCEAN

Columbus, 1492

AFRICA

Henry VII
King of England

Ysabella
Queen of Spain

Manuel I
King of Portugal

Cabot's ship, the bark Matthew, was smaller than the Niña.

John Cabot Lost at Sea
Cabot took ninety-three days to reach the North American coast from England, about twenty days longer than it took Columbus to reach San Salvador. He always believed that the coastline he explored was part of Cathay (China). He made a second voyage in 1498 and was never heard from again.

AMERIGO VESPUCCI, 1454–1512
Italian Explorer in the Service of Spain and Portugal

Amerigo Vespucci was one of the few explorers who was not sent to look for a route to the East. Instead, King Ferdinand and Queen Ysabella of Spain instructed Vespucci to retrace Columbus's journey and find out just what lands Columbus had discovered. Vespucci went north along the Atlantic coast. Two years later, at the request of King Manuel of Portugal, he went south along the same coastline, overlapping some of Columbus's journey.

Vespucci's contribution to the golden age of exploration was immense. During his trips, he took many notes about celestial navigation, astronomy, the new constellations he saw, and the indigenous people and their customs and architecture. But, most importantly, he figured out that the land he had reached was too far south to be either the Indies or Cathay. Therefore, it had to be a new land—but just how big this land was, no one yet knew.

After his voyages were complete, Vespucci wrote a now-famous letter calling the land he had discovered *Mundus Novus*—the New World. The name spread quickly throughout Europe.

"Signore Vespucci, I am sorry to tell you that no statue has ever been erected to you in North or South America in recognition of your discovery."

German Mapmaker Names Continent After the Wrong Explorer!

Martin Waldseemüller made the first accurate map of the New World from Vespucci's journals. Accepting Vespucci's claims of discovery, Waldseemüller named the continent America—after Vespucci's first name. Just think what would have happened if he'd named it after Columbus, who was there before Vespucci!

Amerigo Vespucci was the first explorer to recognize that the land he saw was not Cathay or the Indies. He was also the explorer after whom America was named.

Ptolemy wrote in the second century about navigation and geography. His book was required reading for all explorers.

VESPUCCI'S NEW WORLD

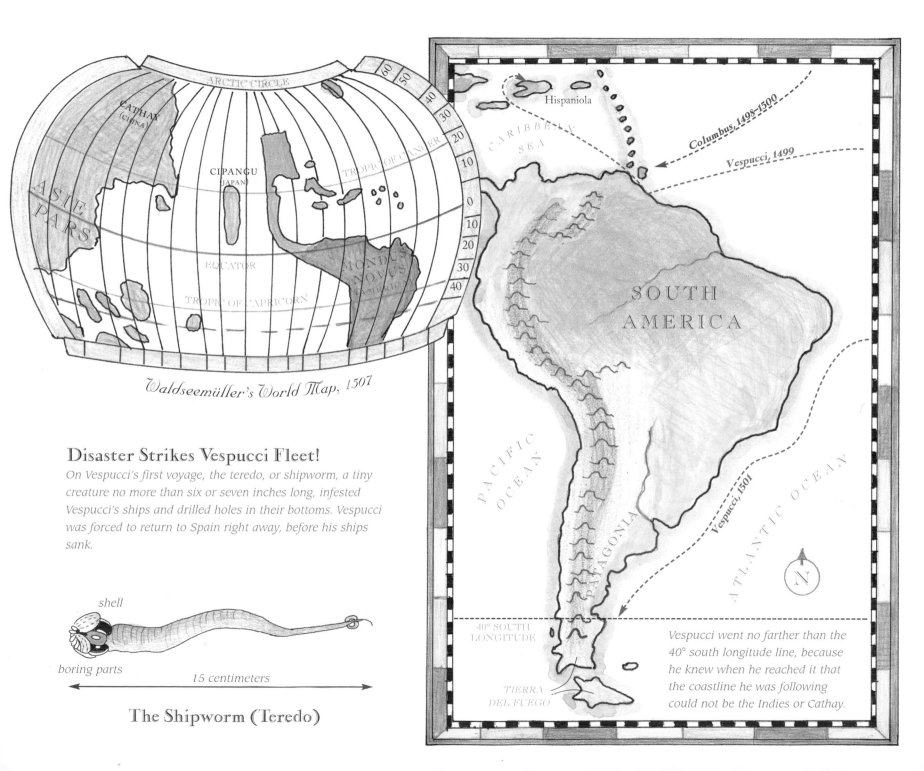

Waldseemüller's World Map, 1507

Disaster Strikes Vespucci Fleet!

On Vespucci's first voyage, the teredo, or shipworm, a tiny creature no more than six or seven inches long, infested Vespucci's ships and drilled holes in their bottoms. Vespucci was forced to return to Spain right away, before his ships sank.

shell

boring parts

← 15 centimeters →

The Shipworm (Teredo)

Vespucci went no farther than the 40° south longitude line, because he knew when he reached it that the coastline he was following could not be the Indies or Cathay.

Vasco Núñez de Balboa, 1475–1519

Spanish Explorer in the Service of Spain

Vasco Núñez de Balboa was an adventurer who liked exploring for its own sake. When he became frustrated by raising pigs in Hispaniola, he stowed away with his dog, Leoncico, on a ship bound for Central America. He landed in Panama and found more than enough adventure in a fever-ridden jungle full of crocodiles, anacondas, jaguars, and scorpions!

Balboa fell in love with the jungle and became very friendly with the local population. He married Anayansi, the daughter of a local Indian chief called Comaco. The chief's son told Balboa about a vast ocean that lay to the west. Balboa, with 190 Spaniards and Indians and Leoncico (Anayansi stayed home), marched west across the Isthmus of Panama and became the first European to see the Pacific Ocean.

Balboa named this ocean the Great South Sea and claimed it for Spain. The discovery proved what many had come to suspect: that there were two oceans and a vast land between Europe and the East.

"¡Buenos días!"

Vasco Núñez de Balboa was a squire to a nobleman, a swordsman, and then a shipbuilder. When he saw the Niña being built, he decided to become an explorer.

"Woof!"

HARINA

Leoncico wore a gold collar.

Flour for the voyage; harina means "flour" in Spanish.

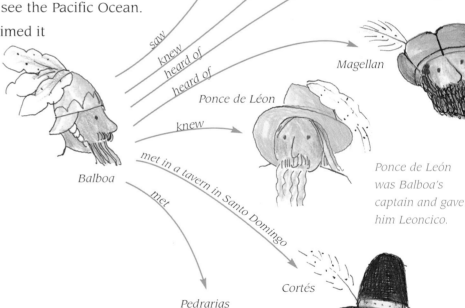

Columbus

de Soto

Cabot

Magellan

saw

knew

heard of

heard of

Ponce de Léon

knew

met in a tavern in Santo Domingo

Balboa

met

Ponce de León was Balboa's captain and gave him Leoncico.

Cortés

Pedrarias

Pedrarias falsely accused Balboa of treason, causing him to be put to death.

**The Explorer's Circle of Friends...
and One Enemy**

10

BALBOA AND ANAYANSI

Anayansi grew up in Panama, a dense jungle full of crocodiles, anacondas, jaguars, scorpions, and monkeys.

Some Indian Civilizations Thriving at the Time of Balboa's Discovery

THE INCA *lived in Peru until 1532, when the Spanish destroyed their empire. They built thousands of miles of paved roads and many bridges and tunnels.*

THE AZTEC *lived in Mexico until 1519, when the Spanish conquered them. They worshiped the sun god and practiced human sacrifice. They also built canals.*

THE MAYA *lived in Mexico and Central America from about 1500 B.C. to A.D. 1526. They built huge cities, studied mathematics and astronomy, and had the only complete written language in Pre-Columbian America.*

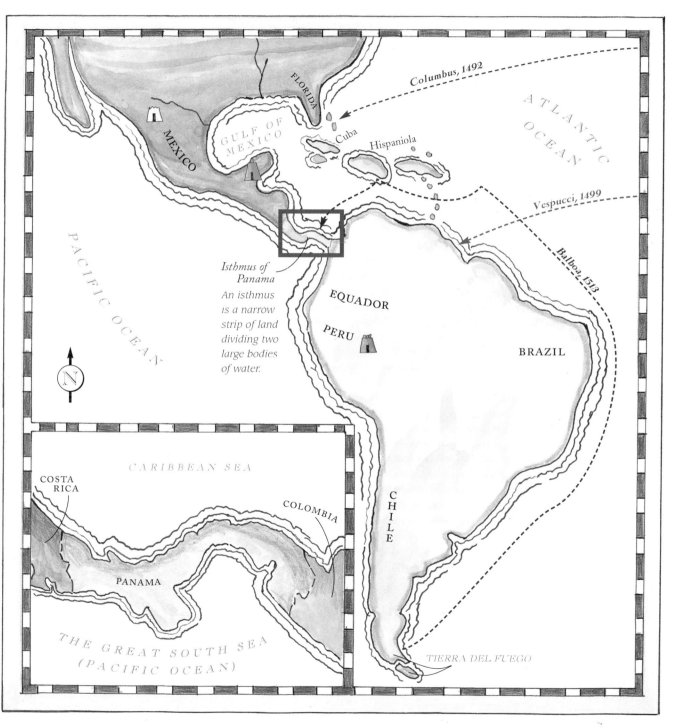

Columbus, 1492

FLORIDA

ATLANTIC OCEAN

GULF OF MEXICO

MEXICO

Cuba

Hispaniola

Vespucci, 1499

Balboa, 1513

Isthmus of Panama
An isthmus is a narrow strip of land dividing two large bodies of water.

PACIFIC OCEAN

N

EQUADOR

PERU

BRAZIL

CHILE

CARIBBEAN SEA

COSTA RICA

COLOMBIA

PANAMA

THE GREAT SOUTH SEA (PACIFIC OCEAN)

TIERRA DEL FUEGO

JUAN PONCE DE LEÓN, 1460–1521

Spanish Explorer in the Service of Spain

Juan Ponce de León was the discoverer of Florida. While in Puerto Rico, which he helped conquer, Ponce de León heard Indian tales of a magical spring that could make old people young again. He set out to find this fountain of youth, but what he found instead was a green and lush land with such beautiful flowers that he called it *La Florida* ("the flower").

Ponce de León believed he was in the Indies, but in fact he was the first European ever to set foot on North America. (John Cabot and his crew had never gone ashore during their North American voyages.) His discovery staked out Spain's claim to this part of the New World, though at that time, Spain was more interested in Central and South America and its gold.

A few years later, Ponce de León was sailing around the Gulf of Mexico and went ashore briefly on the Yucatán Peninsula. Little did he know that just beyond the shoreline of dense tropical trees lay the temples of the great Mayan Empire, a civilization that had thrived in Central America for thousands of years and whose golden treasures would soon dazzle other explorers.

A Sanibel Indian

Bercerillo, infamous fighting dog of Ponce de León, terrorized local populations.

Ponce de León *means "brave lion" in Spanish.*

PONCE DE LEÓN'S FLORIDA

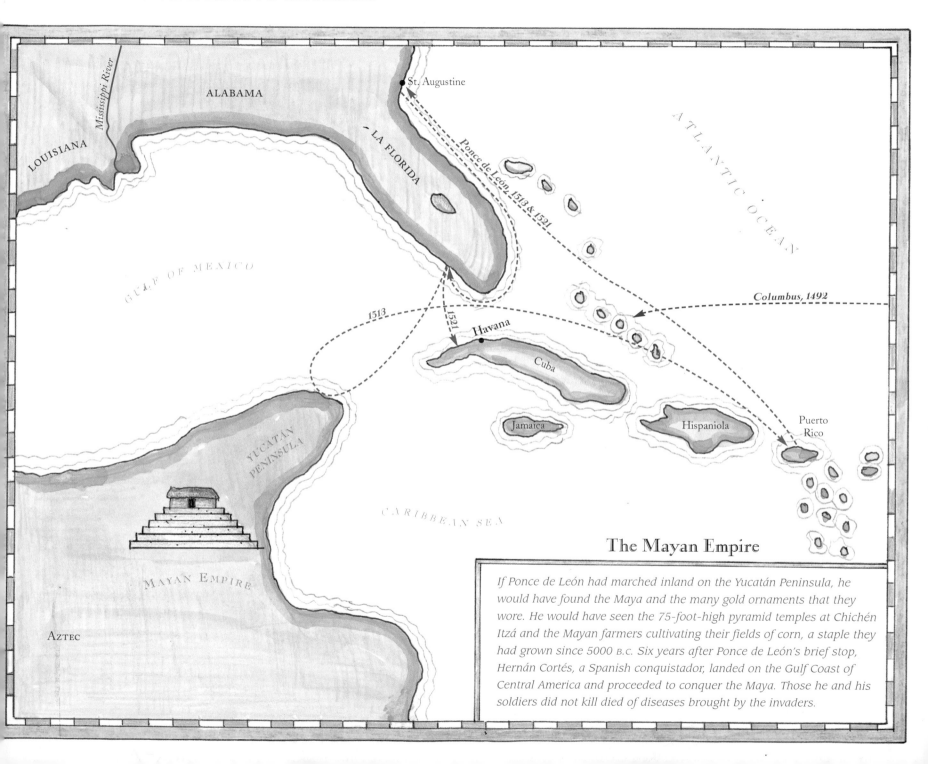

ATLANTIC OCEAN

St. Augustine

ALABAMA

LA FLORIDA

LOUISIANA

Mississippi River

GULF OF MEXICO

Ponce de León 1513 & 1521

Columbus, 1492

1513

1521

Havana

Cuba

Jamaica

Hispaniola

Puerto Rico

YUCATÁN PENINSULA

CARIBBEAN SEA

MAYAN EMPIRE

AZTEC

The Mayan Empire

If Ponce de León had marched inland on the Yucatán Peninsula, he would have found the Maya and the many gold ornaments that they wore. He would have seen the 75-foot-high pyramid temples at Chichén Itzá and the Mayan farmers cultivating their fields of corn, a staple they had grown since 5000 B.C. Six years after Ponce de León's brief stop, Hernán Cortés, a Spanish conquistador, landed on the Gulf Coast of Central America and proceeded to conquer the Maya. Those he and his soldiers did not kill died of diseases brought by the invaders.

FERDINAND MAGELLAN, 1480?–1521

Portuguese Explorer in the Service of Spain

Despite Vespucci's discovery that a huge landmass lay between Europe and the East, the desire to find a direct sea route to the Indies was hard to give up. So King Charles I of Spain sent Ferdinand Magellan on a voyage to sail west *around* the New World to reach the East.

Ferdinand Magellan, with five old ships and a stolen globe covered with the most up-to-date geographical information, did what no other man had ever done: He proved that a ship could circle the world! Sailing west from Spain, he eventually reached the island of Cebu (in the Philippines). He knew that it had been visited by Europeans sailing from the other direction, so he realized that the world could be circled in a ship. He also discovered the strait at the very southern tip of South America that allowed ships to sail from the Atlantic Ocean to the Pacific Ocean.

The 43,380-mile voyage around the world was extremely long and grueling. The rats on the ships devoured much of the ships' stores, and the crew had to eat sawdust and leather strips to stay alive. In fact, Magellan died in the Philippine Islands before the voyage was complete. Only one ship, the *Victoria*, returned home to Spain, with just eighteen sailors aboard.

Trinidad
captured by the Portuguese on the journey home

Santiago
wrecked in a storm off South America

San Antonio
crew mutinied near the Strait of Magellan

Concepción
abandoned in the Philippines

Victoria
completed voyage around the world!

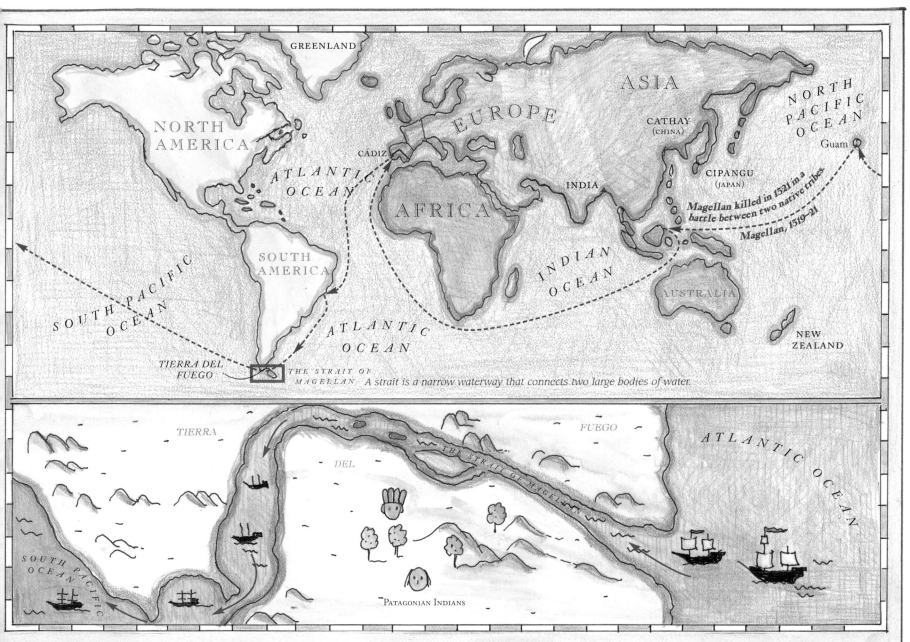

GREENLAND

NORTH AMERICA

ATLANTIC OCEAN

CÁDIZ

EUROPE

ASIA

AFRICA

CATHAY (CHINA)

INDIA

CIPANGU (JAPAN)

NORTH PACIFIC OCEAN

Guam

Magellan killed in 1521 in a battle between two native tribes.

Magellan, 1519–21

SOUTH PACIFIC OCEAN

SOUTH AMERICA

INDIAN OCEAN

AUSTRALIA

NEW ZEALAND

TIERRA DEL FUEGO

THE STRAIT OF MAGELLAN

A strait is a narrow waterway that connects two large bodies of water.

TIERRA

DEL

FUEGO

ATLANTIC OCEAN

THE STRAIT OF MAGELLAN

SOUTH PACIFIC OCEAN

Patagonian Indians

GLOBE THIEF NEVER CAUGHT! *Only a few people knew that a German-made globe covered with the most up-to-date geographical information was on board the Trinidad; it had been stolen from the Portuguese national archives.*

GIOVANNI DA VERRAZANO, 1485?–1528?

Italian Explorer in the Service of France

While Spain was trying to find a way *around* the New World to get to the East, King Francis I of France decided to send Giovanni da Verrazano to find a route *through* the New World.

Verrazano ended up off the coast of North Carolina. He stayed on board writing pages and pages of notes about the land he saw from his ship. Had he left the deck of his ship and ventured inland, he could have claimed valuable land for France. But he was looking for a river that cut through North America, and so continued to travel north along the coast. He discovered New York Bay. The recently built bridge at the entrance to the bay is called the Verrazano-Narrows Bridge in his honor. Further north, he sailed into an inlet along the coast of Rhode Island, discovering the fish-filled Narragansett Bay. He then continued on to the colder climes of Newfoundland before returning home—mission unaccomplished. But he made many wonderful drawings from his travels of the plants and animals and native people he had seen.

Verrazano's first voyage filled in the North American coastline between Cabot's Newfoundland and Ponce de León's Florida. Later explorers concentrated on South America and what mysteries lay *inside* the two continents.

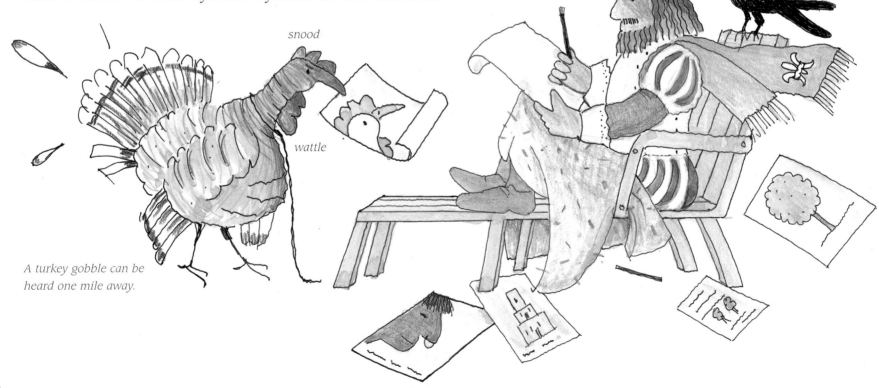

"Awk!"

snood

wattle

A turkey gobble can be heard one mile away.

Big, Bustling Cities in 1528

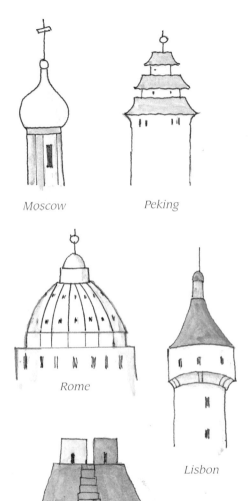

Moscow

Peking

Rome

Lisbon

Tenochtitlán
(Mexico City)

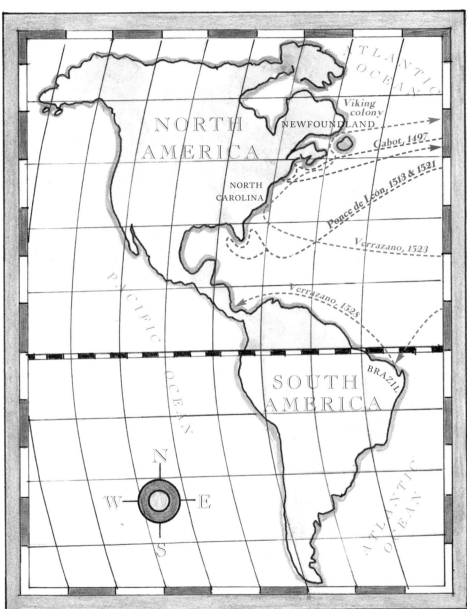

Cities Not Yet Around

New York

Berlin

Tokyo

Verrazano made a second voyage to the New World five years after his first one, still looking for the ever-elusive route to Cathay. This time he went via Brazil. When that search failed, he sailed up the coast of South America hoping to find the sea route to the Indies. He never returned from that voyage. Some believe he was captured by the Cuna Indians, who lived on the Isthmus of Panama.

ALVAR NÚÑEZ CABEZA DE VACA, 1490?–1560?

Spanish Explorer in the Service of Spain

Alvar Núñez Cabeza de Vaca, a soldier, did not intend to explore anything. Instead, he had been sent by King Charles I of Spain to North America to find gold. Everything went wrong. Some of the crew deserted the expedition, and one ship was sunk in a storm. When Cabeza de Vaca (the name means "cow's head" in Spanish) and others finally landed in Florida, they were separated from their ships and quickly ran out of provisions. Starving, they built rafts to escape to Mexico, but many, including Cabeza de Vaca, were then shipwrecked on an island in the Gulf of Mexico.

Months later, Cabeza de Vaca crossed over to the mainland and tried to reach Mexico by foot. More bad luck. Lost, he met up with friendly Indians and traveled with them for more than a year. Eventually he found three of his old comrades: Captain Alonso del Castillo Maldonado; Estevanico, a Muslim slave; and Captain Andrés Dorantes de Carranza, all of whom had been living as slaves of various hostile Indian tribes in Texas. The four escaped and began a long walk. They finally reached Mexico City in 1536. It was one of the longest walks ever—more than two thousand miles. Cabeza de Vaca's book, *Cabeza de Vaca's Adventures in the Unknown Interior of America*, published in Spain in 1542, gave Europeans an idea of just how big this New World was.

Captain Andrés Dorantes de Carranza

Estevanico, a Muslim slave

Captain Alonso del Castillo Maldonado

Cabeza de Vaca, captain general of the expedition, started the myth of the seven golden cities of Cíbola.

Karankawa Indian

CABEZA DE VACA'S VERY LONG WALK

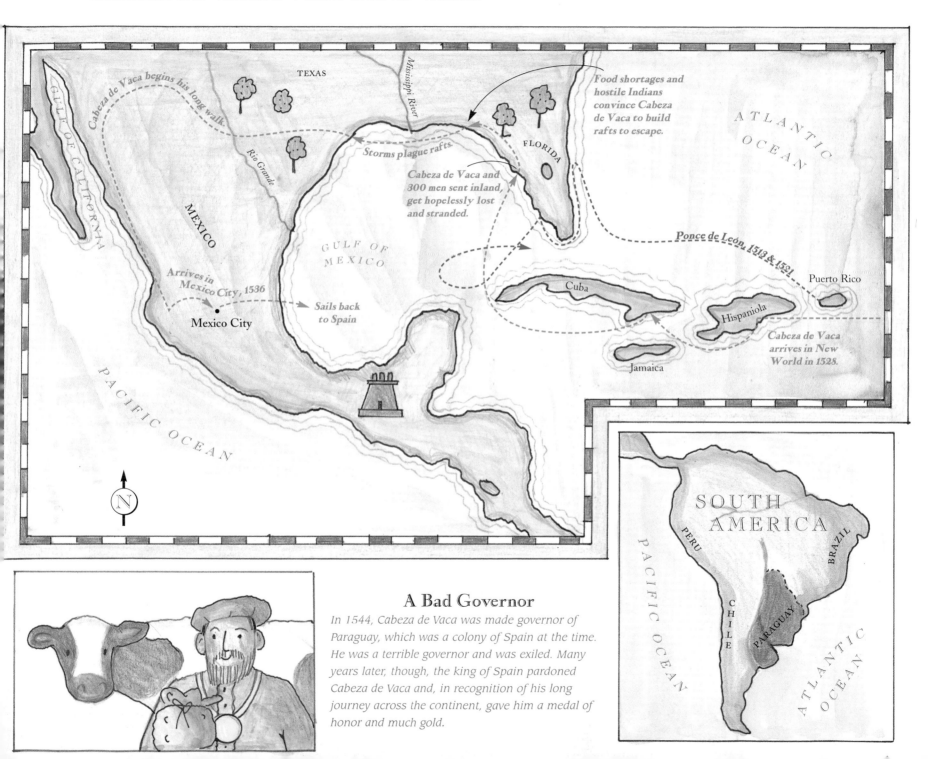

Cabeza de Vaca begins his long walk.

TEXAS

Mississippi River

Food shortages and hostile Indians convince Cabeza de Vaca to build rafts to escape.

ATLANTIC OCEAN

GULF OF CALIFORNIA

Rio Grande

Storms plague rafts.

FLORIDA

Cabeza de Vaca and 300 men sent inland, get hopelessly lost and stranded.

MEXICO

GULF OF MEXICO

Ponce de León, 1513 & 1521

Puerto Rico

Arrives in Mexico City, 1536

Cuba

Sails back to Spain

Hispaniola

Mexico City

Cabeza de Vaca arrives in New World in 1528.

Jamaica

PACIFIC OCEAN

N

A Bad Governor

In 1544, Cabeza de Vaca was made governor of Paraguay, which was a colony of Spain at the time. He was a terrible governor and was exiled. Many years later, though, the king of Spain pardoned Cabeza de Vaca and, in recognition of his long journey across the continent, gave him a medal of honor and much gold.

SOUTH AMERICA

PERU

BRAZIL

CHILE

PARAGUAY

PACIFIC OCEAN

ATLANTIC OCEAN

JACQUES CARTIER, 1491-1557
French Explorer in the Service of France

Miffed at the Spanish and Portuguese claiming all the land in the New World, King Francis I of France rumbled, "The sun shines for me, too!" Then he sent Jacques Cartier to join the search.

On his first voyage, Cartier made landfall on the far northeast coast of North America and found himself at the mouth of the great St. Lawrence River. He poked around the nearby islands and then sailed home. On his second and third trips, he took small boats to the same area and ventured 1,600 miles upriver into the continent. Like Verrazano, Cartier was looking for a passage to the Pacific Ocean. What he found instead was a vast land of dense forests, inland bays, and tribes of the Iroquois and Micmac. He claimed this huge section of northeastern Canada for France. The French would wait sixty years before sending another explorer to the New World (his name was Samuel de Champlain).

egret feather

ostrich plume

eagle feather

King Francis I sends Cartier to find the Northwest Passage.

Cartier finds lots of fish instead. He also brings back two Iroquois Indians for the French court to see.

Micmac Indians bring furs to the French in exchange for guns. Sixty years later the French realize that there is a fortune to be made in furs and set out to colonize Canada.

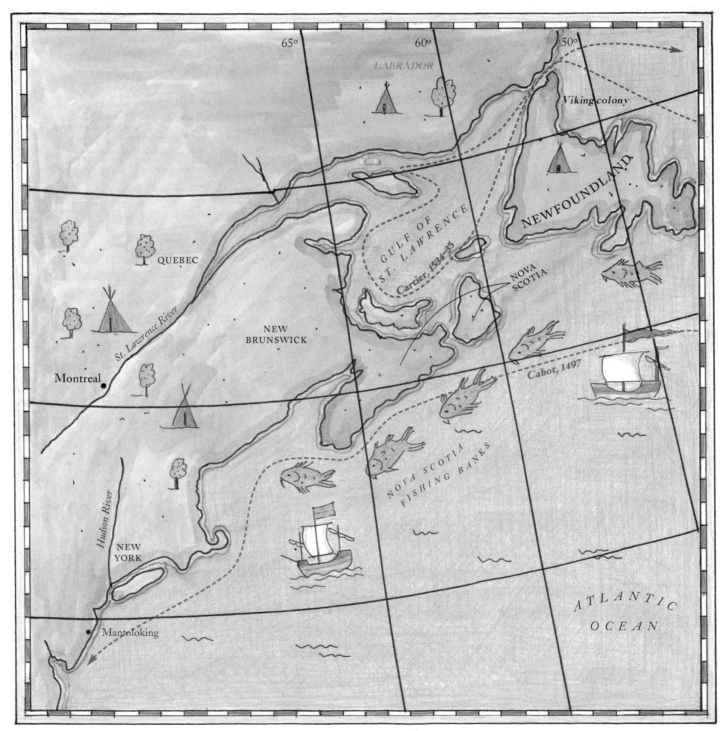

65° 60° 50°

LABRADOR

Viking colony

GULF OF ST. LAWRENCE

Cartier, 1534-35

NEWFOUNDLAND

QUEBEC

NOVA SCOTIA

St. Lawrence River

NEW BRUNSWICK

Montreal

Cabot, 1497

Hudson River

NOVA SCOTIA FISHING BANKS

NEW YORK

ATLANTIC OCEAN

Mantoloking

HERNANDO DE SOTO, 1500?–1542

Spanish Explorer in the Service of Spain

By the early 1500s Spain was turning its attention to what riches the New World could offer. Having conquered Central and South America, King Charles I of Spain decided to move into North America. He sent Hernando de Soto to conquer *La Florida* and see if he could find the fabled Seven Cities of Cíbola, which were rumored to be built of gold.

The Seven Legendary Cities of Cíbola

Conquistador is the name used for any of the sixteenth-century Spanish conquerors in America.

De Soto, along with 600 soldiers and horses, landed in *La Florida* and began a systematic destruction of the Apalachee tribe. They continued a bloody march across southeastern North America that wended through the lands of the Choctaw, Cherokee, and Creek Indians.

As a conquistador, de Soto was cruel and ruthless. As an explorer, he went farther into the North American continent than any other European. He is best known for being the first European to come upon one of the longest rivers in the world. De Soto called it the Rio de Spiritus, but it already had a Chippewa name: the Mississippi, or Great River.

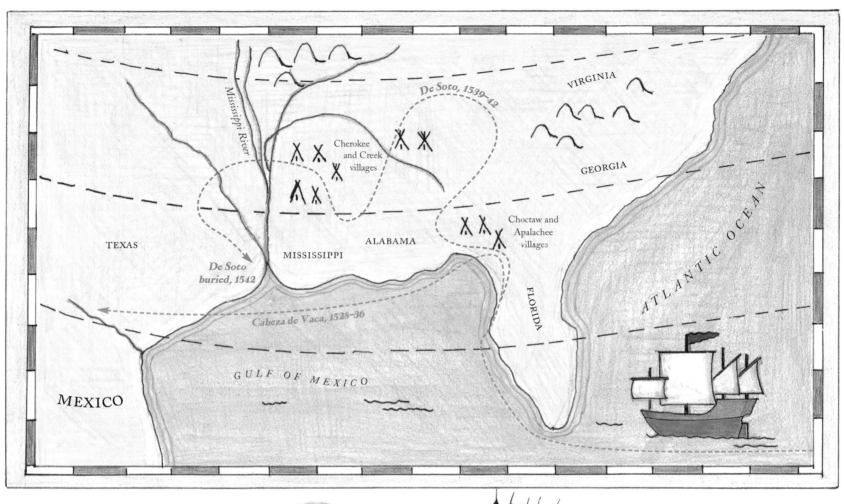

King Charles I, grandson of Ferdinand and Ysabella, ruled that Indians could not be made slaves, so de Soto simply killed all the Indians he met.

Tuscaloosa, Choctaw leader, attacked de Soto's troops and drove them north, where de Soto stumbled upon the Mississippi River.

Francisco Vásquez de Coronado, 1510?–1554

Spanish Explorer in the Service of Spain

Despite de Soto's failure to find anything resembling the Seven Cities of Cíbola, Francisco Vásquez de Coronado was sent on the same fruitless expedition. It wasn't all King Charles's doing; Coronado was just as eager to find the cities of gold and even sank his entire life savings into the expedition. He assembled a hoard of men and beasts for the journey and set out from New Spain.

Alas, his trip was no more successful than de Soto's. The fact was, there was no Cíbola. However, Coronado's journey filled in the southwestern lands of North America. He marched though the deserts of Arizona and New Mexico, and the Great Plains of present-day Oklahoma and Kansas, and he saw the glorious pueblos of the Zuni and the thatched huts of the Plains Indians. Some of Coronado's soldiers were also the first Europeans to see one of the seven natural wonders of the world—the Grand Canyon.

herd of mules

1,000 Indian scouts and slaves

friars

horses and cattle (mustangs are descendants of these horses)

Coronado, the leader, age 30

herd of sheep

336 Spanish officers and soldiers

CORONADO'S QUEST FOR GOLD

*thatched huts
of the Plains Indians*

*pueblos
of the Zuni Indians*

1598 Map Showing the Location of the Seven Cities of Cibola

(Septem Civitatum Patria)

SEPTEM
CIVITATUM
PATRIA
GRANA
TA
NOVA
CALIFORNIA
CALIFORNIA SINUS
TROPICUS CAPRICORNI
OCEANUS OCCIDENTALIS SIVE
PACIFICUM MARE

CALIFORNIA

NEVADA

Grand
Canyon

ARIZONA

Colorado River

Plains Indian
Lands

KANSAS

Arkansas River

OKLAHOMA

Zuni Lands

NEW MEXICO

Rio Grande

Mississippi River

De Soto, 1539–42

ALABAMA

MISSISSIPPI

Coronado, 1540

PACIFIC OCEAN

GULF OF CALIFORNIA

NEW
SPAIN

Cabeza de Vaca, 1528–36

FLORIDA

GULF OF MEXICO

JUAN RODRÍGUEZ CABRILLO, 1500?–1543

Portuguese Explorer in the Service of Spain

João Rodrigues Cabrilho, now known as Juan Rodriguez Cabrillo, is not as famous as some of the other explorers in this book. But his explorations filled in lands on the California coast, the last remaining coastline to be explored by Europeans in the Americas.

At the request of the viceroy of New Spain, Cabrillo set out to see what lands lay at the edge of the Pacific. After a false start or two, Cabrillo sailed north to present-day San Diego, in and out of harbors and bays, until he reached what is now Point Reyes, fifty miles north of San Francisco. There Cabrillo must have seen sheer cliffs and pounding surf, and he must have marveled at the 450 species of birds, such as the albatross, the brant, and the snowy plover.

With Cabrillo's death, the golden age of exploration was more or less over. The stage was now set for the most powerful kingdoms in Europe to fight bloody wars over their newfound lands. And just 350 years after Columbus waded ashore in North America looking for gold, gold was discovered in California, by Americans.

"Awk!"

brant

Cabrillo *means* "goat" *in Spanish.*

Cabrillo's Fatal Step

While on Santa Cruz Island of Southern California, Cabrillo stumbled upon the Miwok Indians. This coastal tribe had been in the area since at least 3000 B.C. They were expert basket and bead makers and lived in cone-shaped houses made from willow branches and covered in grasses.

Cabrillo tripped while being chased by the Miwok and hit his head on a rock. He died later on the San Miguel Islands off the coast of Santa Barbara.

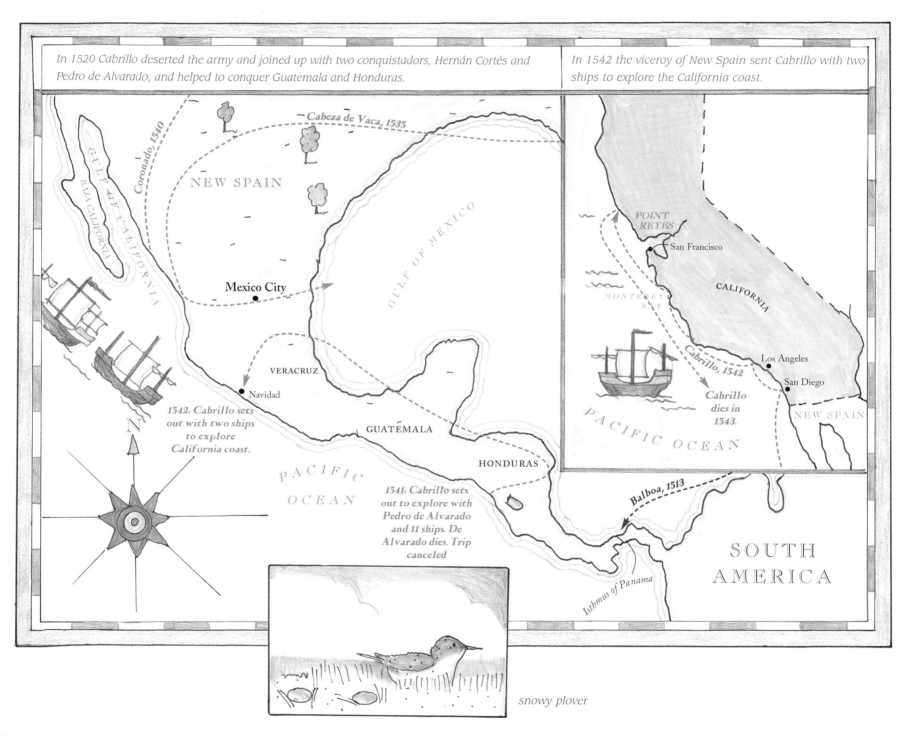

In 1520 Cabrillo deserted the army and joined up with two conquistadors, Hernán Cortés and Pedro de Alvarado, and helped to conquer Guatemala and Honduras.

In 1542 the viceroy of New Spain sent Cabrillo with two ships to explore the California coast.

Coronado 1540

Cabeza de Vaca, 1535

NEW SPAIN

GULF OF CALIFORNIA

BAJA CALIFORNIA

GULF OF MEXICO

Mexico City

POINT REYES

San Francisco

CALIFORNIA

MONTEREY BAY

Los Angeles

Cabrillo, 1542

San Diego

VERACRUZ

Navidad

1542: Cabrillo sets out with two ships to explore California coast.

Cabrillo dies in 1543.

NEW SPAIN

N

PACIFIC OCEAN

GUATEMALA

HONDURAS

PACIFIC OCEAN

1541: Cabrillo sets out to explore with Pedro de Alvarado and 11 ships. De Alvarado dies. Trip canceled

Balboa, 1513

SOUTH AMERICA

Isthmus of Panama

snowy plover

~ The World After the Explorers ~

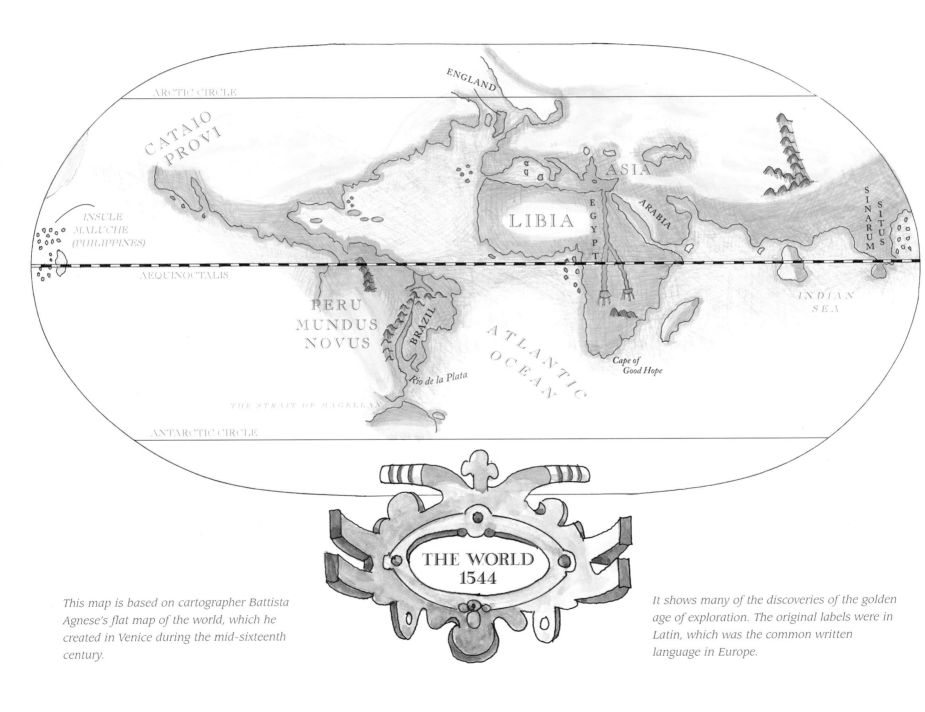

ENGLAND

ARCTIC CIRCLE

CATAIO PROVI

ASIA

INSULE MALUCHE (PHILIPPINES)

LIBIA

EGYPT

ARABIA

SINARUM SITUS

AEQUINOCTALIS

PERU MUNDUS NOVUS

BRAZIL

ATLANTIC OCEAN

Cape of Good Hope

INDIAN SEA

Rio de la Plata

THE STRAIT OF MAGELLAN

ANTARCTIC CIRCLE

THE WORLD 1544

This map is based on cartographer Battista Agnese's flat map of the world, which he created in Venice during the mid-sixteenth century.

It shows many of the discoveries of the golden age of exploration. The original labels were in Latin, which was the common written language in Europe.

A Note from the Author

Writing and illustrating history books is a dream come true. I love to draw ships with sails, flags, maps, elaborate costumes, feathered bonnets, lace collars, and funny shoes. And I love research.

Of course, it can be a challenge sometimes to find out the "real" facts. No one knows for sure if Columbus had a clean-shaven face or a long pointy beard, or if there were pigs on board the *Santa Maria*, because the events happened so long ago.

History is an inexact science. Not only are there facts to be uncovered, but those facts themselves can be interpreted in many ways. For centuries, the twelve explorers in this book were hailed as heroes for discovering the New World. It's only in the last century that we have come to realize the high price of their exploration: the decimation of the Indian tribes and their cultures through battle and exposure to disease.

I have read and studied many books to bring this one to you in as true and real a way as I could. I tried to present the high hopes of the explorers and some of the bad luck and misfortunes they encountered. I have also relied on old, inaccurate maps to convey what the explorers themselves might have been looking at as they sailed their ships over unknown seas and rode their horses through uncharted lands.

INDEX

Anayansi, 10, 11
Apalachee, 22, 23
Atlantic Ocean, 5, 7, 9, 11, 13, 14, 15, 17, 21, 28
Aztec, 11, 13

Bahamas, 4, 5
Balboa, Vasco Núñez de, 3, 10–11, 27
Brazil, 11, 17, 28

Cabeza de Vaca, Alvar Núñez, 3, 18–19, 23, 25, 27
Cabot, John, 2, 6–7, 10, 12, 16, 17, 21
Cabrillo, Juan Rodríguez, 3, 26–27
California, 25, 26, 27
Canada, 7, 20
Cartier, Jacques, 2, 20–21
Cathay, 4, 5, 7, 8, 9, 15, 17. *See also* China
Central America, 10, 11, 12, 13, 22
Champlain, Samuel de, 20
Charles I, king of Spain, 14, 18, 22, 23, 24
Cherokee, 22, 23
China, 4, 5, 7, 9, 15. *See also* Cathay
Choctaw, 22, 23
Cíbola, 18, 22, 24, 25
Columbus, Christopher, 3, 4–5, 6, 7, 8, 9, 10, 11, 13, 26
conquistadors, 22, 27
Coronado, Francisco Vásquez de, 3, 24–25, 27
Cortés, Hernán, 10, 13, 27
Creek (Indians), 22, 23
Cuba, 5, 11, 13, 19

de Soto, Hernando, 3, 10, 22–23, 24, 25

England, 4, 28
Eriksson, Leif, 2

Ferdinand, king of Spain, 4, 8, 23
Florida, 5, 11, 12, 16, 18, 19, 23, 25. *See also La Florida*
France, 16, 20
Francis I, king of France, 16, 20

gold, 2, 6, 18, 19, 22, 24, 26
Grand Banks, 6, 7
Grand Canyon, 24, 25
Great South Sea, 10, 11. *See also* Pacific Ocean

Henry VII, king of England, 6, 7
Hispaniola, 5, 9, 10, 11, 13, 19

Inca, 11
Iroquois, 20
Isabella, queen of Spain. *See* Ysabella

Jamaica, 5, 13, 19

La Florida, 12, 13, 22

Magellan, Ferdinand, 3, 10, 14–15
Manuel I, king of Portugal, 7, 8
maps, world
  Agnese, 27
  Waldseemüller, 9
Maya, 11, 13
Mayan Empire, 12, 13
Mexico, 11, 18, 19, 23
Mexico, Gulf of, 11, 12, 13, 18, 19, 23, 25, 27
Mexico City, 17, 18, 19, 27
Micmac, 20
Mississippi River, 13, 19, 22, 23, 25
Miwok, 26
Mundus Novus, 8, 9, 28. *See also* New World

Newfoundland, 6, 16, 17, 21
New Jersey, 6, 7
New Mexico, 24, 25
New Spain, 24, 25, 26, 27
New World, 8, 12, 14, 16, 17, 18, 20, 22. *See also Mundus Novus*
New York, 16, 21
Niña, 4, 10
North America, 2, 4, 5, 6, 7, 8, 12, 15, 16, 17, 18, 20, 22, 24, 26
Nova Scotia, 6, 7, 21

Pacific Ocean, 2, 10, 11, 14, 15, 17, 19, 20, 25, 26, 27
Panama, 10, 11
Panama, Isthmus of, 11, 17, 27
Pedrarias, 10
Peru, 11, 19, 28
Philippines, 14, 28
Pinta, 4
Pinzón, Martín, 4
Pinzón, Vicente, 4
Plains (Indians), 24, 25
Polo, Marco, 5, 6
Ponce de León, Juan, 3, 10, 12–13, 16, 17, 19
Portugal, 7, 8
Puerto Rico, 12, 13, 19

San Salvador, 5, 7
Santa Cruz Island, 26
Santa Maria, 4
shipworm, 9
South America, 2, 5, 8, 9, 14, 15, 16, 17, 22, 27
Spain, 4, 7, 8, 10, 12, 14, 16, 18, 19, 22, 24, 26
St. Lawrence River, 20, 21
Strait of Magellan, 15, 28

Texas, 18, 19, 23
Tierra del Fuego, 9, 11, 15
Trinidad, 5
Tuscaloosa, 23

Verrazano, Giovanni da, 2, 15, 16–17, 20
Vespucci, Amerigo, 3, 8–9, 11, 14
Victoria, 14
Vikings, 2, 5, 6, 7, 17, 21

Waldseemüller, Martin, 8, 9

Ysabella, queen of Spain, 4, 7, 8, 23
Yucatán Peninsula, 12, 13

Zuni, 24, 25

THE EXPLORERS AT SEA

Ship's Stores on the Magellan Fleet of 1519

(to last 230 men on five ships two years)

989 cheeses

CARNE DE PUERCO

5,700 pounds dried pork
(packed in brine)

6,100 pounds beans, lentils, chickpeas

5,600 pounds vinegar

1,512 pounds honey in jars

15 tons biscuits

322 pounds rice

SAILOR'S PERSONAL EFFECTS

earthenware soup bowl

drinking horn

plate

knife

spoon

525 pounds flour

100 pounds mustard

DAY MEAL
onion
fish
biscuit

ceramic water jug for crew

sea chest

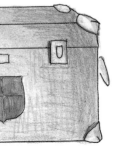

HIGOS

16 casks figs

sailor on fifteenth-century ship

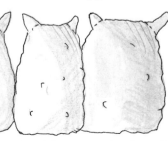

450 strings garlic
and onion

3,200 pounds raisins, currants, almonds